Handy Utah Genealogy Handbook

Gary L. Morris

ISBN-13: 978-1508430292

ISBN-10: 1508430292

Table of Contents

Notes

Genealogical Research in Utah

Because of its long and eventful history, there are many historical and genealogical records and resources available for tracing your family history in Utah. Many even call Utah the "Hub of American Genealogy." Because of the abundance of information held at many different locations, tracking down the records for your ancestor can be an ominous task. Don't worry though, we know just where they are, and we'll show you which records you'll need, while helping you to understand:

1. What they are
2. Where to find them
3. How to use them

These records can be found both online and off, so we'll introduce you to online websites, indexes and databases, as well as brick-and-mortar repositories and other institutions that will help with your research in Utah. So that you will have a more comprehensive understanding of these records, we have provided a brief history of the "Beehive State" to illustrate what type of records may have been generated during specific time periods. That information will assist you in pinpointing times and locations on which to focus the search for your Utah ancestors and their records.

A Brief History of Utah

Utah's primary Indian groups are Shoshonean: the Goshute of the western desert, the Ute in the eastern two-thirds of the state, and the Southern Paiute of southwestern Utah. The differing lifestyles of each tribe remained basically unchanged until the horse was introduced by the Spanish sometime after 1600. White settlement beginning in 1847 led to two wars between whites and the Native American tribes-the Walker War of 1853–54 and the even bloodier Black Hawk War of 1865–68, which resulted in the final removal of many Indians to reservations.

Spaniards and Mexicans are the first non-Native Americans known to have entered Utah, with Juan María Antonio Rivera reputedly arriving near modern-day Moab as early as 1765. In 1776 Franciscan priests entered Utah from the east and traversed the Uinta basin, crossed the Wasatch Mountains, and spent time at the Ute encampment at Utah Lake. Trade between Santa Fe, and the Native American tribes of Utah was well established by the early 1800s.

The Spanish Trail, the longest segment of which lies in Utah, was the primary route through the Southwest until 1848. Many mountain men followed this rout to the region in search of furs, and brought settlers and explorers en route to California. Once such group of settlers was the Mormons, who decided to head west after their leader Joseph Smith was lynched at Carthage, Illinois, in June of 1844. Arriving at Salt Lake Valley on July 22, they began planting and irrigating immediately.

At the end of the Mexican-American war, the Treaty of Guadalupe-Hidalgo (1848) gave the United States title to a vast amount of the Southwest. At this time the Mormons established a provisional state they named Deseret. Deseret was not recognized by the federal government, who decided to create the Utah Territory instead. Utah territory consisted if all of present day Utah, as well as parts of Wyoming, Colorado, and Nevada. The present day borders of Utah were established in 1860 following land cessions.

The forty six years of the Territorial period saw much growth, conflict, and immigration. It was during this time that the darkest event in Utah history occurred. Rumors that Utahans were rebelling against federal authority caused then President James Buchanan to send an expeditionary force to investigate in 1857. On 11 September, caught up in an atmosphere of war hysteria, Mormon militiamen and their Indian allies massacred over 100 California-bound migrants at Mountain Meadows. Peace was restored in June 1858, and Brigham Young was replaced by Alfred Cumming as territorial governor. Cumming's appointment sparked the beginning of sustained hostility between Mormon leaders and the federal government.

Up until 1870 98% of the population of Utah was Mormon. The Mormon lifestyle dominated economics, politics, and cultural and social activities. Although no longer governor, Brigham Young was the principal figure in Utah until his death in 1877. In the decade before his death he had contracted Union Pacific to lay some of the track for the transcontinental railroad in the state, and on May 10, 1869, the Union and Central Pacific Railroads were joined at Promontory. New rail lines also connected to the capitol, Salt Lake City, and in 1863 when silver was re-discovered, a mining boom began.

Important Dates in Utah History

1847 – First Mormons arrive in Salt Lake Valley; Provisional government set up by Mormon Church
1848 – Acquired from Mexico in Treaty of Guadalupe-Hidalgo
1849 – State of Deseret created
1850 – Organized as Utah Territory
1852 – Iron mine established near Cedar City
1857 – Utah War
1862 – Congress makes polygamy illegal in all US territories
1865 – Ute-Blackhawk War
1895 – Constitution drafted
1896 – Statehood

Famous Battles Fought in Utah

Utah was not the scene of any fighting during the Revolutionary and Civil Wars, but two other important wars took place on Utah soil; the **Utah War** in 1857, and the **Ute-Blackhawk War** in 1865.

The battle accounts that exist can be very effective in uncovering the military records of your ancestor. They can tell you what regiments fought in which battles, and often include the names and ranks of many officers and enlisted men.

Utah War: https://www.lds.org/manual/church-history-in-the-fulness-of-times-student-manual/chapter-twenty-nine-the-utah-war?lang=eng

Ute-Blackhawk War:
http://content.lib.utah.edu/cdm/ref/collection/upcat/id/1428

Common Utah Genealogical Issues and Resources to Overcome Them

Boundary Changes: Boundary changes are a common obstacle when researching Utah ancestors. You could be searching for an ancestor's record in one county when in fact it is stored in a different one due to historical county boundary changes.

The **Atlas of Historical County Boundaries** can help you to overcome that problem. It provides a chronological listing of every boundary change that has occurred in the history of Utah.

Atlas of Historical County Boundaries:
http://publications.newberry.org/ahcbp/documents/UT_Consolidated
_Chronology.htm#Consolidated_Chronology

Name Changes: Surname changes, variations, and misspellings can complicate genealogical research. It is important to check all spelling variations. Soundex, a program that indexes names by sound, is a useful first step, but you can't rely on it completely as some name variations result in different Soundex codes. The surnames could be different, but the first name may be different too. You can also find records filed under initials, middle names, and nicknames as well, so you will need to **get creative with surname variations** and spellings in order to cover all the possibilities. For help with surname variations read our instructional article on **How to Use Soundex**.

get creative with surname variations:
http://obituarieshelp.org/blog/?p=634

How to Use Soundex: http://obituarieshelp.org/blog/?p=505

Utah Genealogical Organizations and Archives

Genealogical resources include not only records, but the organizations that house them, or can direct you to them. These institutions include: *Archives, Libraries, Genealogical Societies, Family History Centers, Universities, Churches, and Museums.*

Following are links to their websites, their physical addresses, and a summary of the records you can find there.

Archives and Libraries

Utah State Archives – Vital records, Land records, Military records, Probate records, Naturalization records, Mining records, Cemetery records

300 S Rio Grande St
Salt Lake City, UT 84101
Tel: (801) 533-3535

Utah State Archives: http://www.archives.state.ut.us

Family Search Family History Library - over 2.4 million rolls of microfilmed genealogical records; 727,000 microfiche; 356,000 books, serials, and other formats; over 4,500 periodicals and 3,725 electronic resources. Includes census records, Immigration and Naturalization records, Court records, vital records, Probate records and Wills, Military records, Land records, Estate records and much more

35 North West Temple Street
Salt Lake City, Utah, 84150
1-866-406-1830

Family History Library:
https://familysearch.org/locations/saltlakecity-library

BYU Family History Library - Bible Records, Census Records, Death & Obituary Records, Immigration Records, Military Records, Probate Records, Vital Records, Miscellaneous Records (Family Trees, Historic journals, etc.)

P.O. Box 26800, Provo, UT 84602-6800
(801) 422-2927

BYU Family History Library:
http://sites.lib.byu.edu/familyhistory/records/

Utah State Library – unique collection of genealogical resources featuring the Pioneer Online Library which features Emigration Registers, the Mormon Pioneer Overland Travel, 1847-1868 database - a searchable listing of individuals and companies in which Mormon pioneer emigrants traveled west to Utah from 1847 through 1868, Ogden City Cemetery records, Utah Death Certificate Index, 1904-[ongoing], and the Western States Marriage Record Index

250 North, 1950 West, Suite A
Salt Lake City, UT 84116-7901
801-715-6777

Utah State Library:
http://pioneer.utah.gov/research/guides/genealogy.html

University of Utah, Willard J. Marriot Library – Manuscripts, Historical newspapers, rare books, Historical maps

Willard J. Marriot Library
295 South 1500
East Salt Lake City, Utah 84112-0860
Tel: (801) 581-8558
Fax: (801) 585-3464

Willard J. Marriot Library:
http://www.lib.utah.edu/collections/special-collections/index.php

Utah State University, Merrill- Cazier Library Special Collections – manuscript collection, historical photographs, historical maps, rare books

Merrill- Cazier Library Special Collections
3000 Old Main Hill
Logan, Utah 84322
Tel: (435) 797-2663

Merrill- Cazier Library Special Collections:
https://library.usu.edu/Specol/

Genealogical and Historical Societies

Genealogical and historical societies have access to extensive catalogues of genealogical data. They are also able to offer expert guidance for genealogical researchers. Many members are professional genealogists who are most willing to share their expertise in finding ancestors.

Utah Genealogical Association – Vast array of genealogical resources for searching Utah ancestors

P.O. Box 1144
Salt Lake City, UT 84110
801-259-4172
Utah Genealogical Association: http://www.infouga.org/

Daughters of the Utah Pioneers – Utah Pioneer Index and vast library containing artifacts, family histories, manuscripts, historical photographs and maps

300 N. Main St.
Salt Lake City, UT 84103-1699
801-532-6479
Daughters of the Utah Pioneers:
http://www.dupinternational.org/index.php

Sons of Utah Pioneers – Manuscripts, Biographies, Family-type history books and biographies, Locality books and histories, military records, Immigration records, Polygamists and time served, Perpetual Emigration Fund Emigrants, Trail Marker Newsletter (Monthly), Pioneer Magazine (Quarterly),

3301 East 2920 South
Salt Lake City, UT 84109
Toll-free Tel: 1-866-724-1847
LocalTel: 801-484-4441
Fax: 801-484-2067
E-mail: sup1847@gmail.com

Sons of Utah Pioneers: http://www.sonsofutahpioneers.org/

Additional Utah Genealogy Resources

Utah Mailing Lists

Mailing lists are internet based facilities that use email to distribute a single message to all who subscribe to it. When information on a particular surname, new records, or any other important genealogy information related to the mailing list topic becomes available, the subscribers are alerted to it. Joining a mailing list is an excellent way to stay up to date on Utah genealogy research topics. Rootsweb have an extensive listing of **Utah Mailing Lists** on a variety of topics.

Utah Mailing Lists:
http://lists.rootsweb.ancestry.com/index/usa/UT/misc.html

Utah Message Boards

A message board is another internet based facility where people can post questions about a specific genealogy topic and have it answered by other genealogists. If you have questions about a surname, record type, or research topic, you can post your question and other researchers and genealogists will help you with the answer. Be sure to check back regularly, as the answers are not emailed to you. The Utah message boards at **Rootsweb** are completely free to use.

Rootsweb:
http://boards.rootsweb.com/localities.northam.usa.states/mb.ashx

Utah Newspapers and Periodicals

Many genealogy periodicals and historical newspapers contain reprinted copies of family genealogies, transcripts of family Bible records, information about local records and archives, census indexes, church records, queries, land records, obituaries, court records, cemetery records, and wills. The following sites have historical Utah newspapers and periodicals that you can search online or on-site.

Utah State Archives – Digital collection of historical newspapers dating from 1870 to late 20th century

300 S Rio Grande St
Salt Lake City, UT 84101
Tel: (801) 533-3535

Utah State Archives: http://digitalnewspapers.org/

Family Search Family History Library - over 4,500 periodicals

35 North West Temple Street
Salt Lake City, Utah, 84150
1-866-406-1830

Family History Library:
https://familysearch.org/locations/saltlakecity-library

GenealogyBank.com – free searchable database of Utah newspaper archives, 1851-1922

GenealogyBank.com:
http://www.genealogybank.com/gbnk/newspapers/explore/USA/Utah/

The Online Books Page – links to historical Utah books and periodicals available for viewing online

The Online Books Page: http://onlinebooks.library.upenn.edu

Library of Congress Digital Newspaper Directory – free searchable database of historical U.S. newspapers dating from 1690-present

Library of Congress Digital Newspaper Directory: http://chroniclingamerica.loc.gov/search/titles/

NewspaperArchive.com – largest online database of historical newspapers in the world.

NewspaperArchive.com: http://newspaperarchive.com/

Historical Utah Maps and Gazetteers

Maps are an integral part of genealogical research. They help us to locate landmarks, towns, cities, parishes, states, provinces, waterways and roads and streets. They also help us to determine when and where boundary changes might have taken place, and give us a visualization of the area we're researching in.

For locating place names, a gazetteer is the best possible resource for any genealogist. Gazetteers are also sometimes called "place name dictionaries", and can help you to locate the area in which you need to conduct research. Below are links to the maps and gazetteers for research in Utah.

Peabody GNIS Service: http://peabody.research.yale.edu/cgi-bin/Query.GNIS?ST=Utah&SU=1

Color Landform Atlas – Utah: http://fermi.jhuapl.edu/states/ut_0.html

1985 U.S. Atlas: http://www.livgenmi.com/1895/UT/

Utah Hometown Locator: http://utah.hometownlocator.com/

Utah City Directories
.

City directories are similar to telephone directories in that they list the residents of a particular area. The difference though is what is important to genealogists, and that is they pre-date telephone directories. You can find an ancestor's information such as their street address, place of employment, occupation, or the name of their spouse. A one-stop-shop for finding city directories in Utah is the **Utah Online Historical Directories** which contains a listing of every available online historical directory related to Utah. Another useful site is **US City Directories** which identifies printed, microfilmed, and online Utah directories and their repositories.

Utah Online Historical Directories:
https://sites.google.com/site/onlinedirectorysite/Home/usa/ut

US City Directories: http://www.uscitydirectories.com/ut.htm

Some archives and libraries that have both digitized and microfilmed city directories for Utah are:

Utah State Archives
300 S Rio Grande St
Salt Lake City, UT 84101
Tel: (801) 533-3535

Utah State Archives: http://www.archives.state.ut.us

University of Utah
J. Willard Marriott Library
295 S 1500 E SLC
UT 84112-0860
Tel: 801.581.8558
Fax: 801.585.3464

J. Willard Marriott Library: http://lib.utah.edu/index

Utah Division of State History

300 S. Rio Grande Street (450 West)
Salt Lake City, UT 84101
Tel. General Number: 801-245-7225
Tel. Research Center: 801-245-7227
Fax. Historical Society: 801-533-3567
Fax. Research Center: 801-533-3504

Utah Division of State History: http://heritage.utah.gov/history

Utah Genealogical Records

Birth, Death, Marriage and Divorce Records – Also known as vital records, birth, death, and marriage certificates are the most basic, yet most important records attached to your ancestor. The reason for their importance is that they not only place your ancestor in a specific place at a definite time, but potentially connect the individual to other relatives. Below is a list of repositories and websites where you can find Utah vital records.

Utah Office of Vital Records and Statistics – Births and Deaths after 1905, Marriage and Divorce post 1978

288 North 1460 West
PO BOX 141012
Salt Lake City, UT 84114-1012
801-538-9467

Utah Office of Vital Records and Statistics:
https://silver.health.utah.gov/index.html

Utah State Archives – Marriage records and licenses 1887- late 20th century, Births 1890-present, Deaths 1848-present, Territorial Divorce records, 1852-1895, County Divorce records 1896-present

300 S Rio Grande St
Salt Lake City, UT 84101
Tel: (801) 533-3535

Utah State Archives: http://www.archives.state.ut.us

Utah State Library – Utah Death Certificate Index, 1904-[ongoing], and the Western States Marriage Record Index

250 North, 1950 West, Suite A
Salt Lake City, UT 84116-7901
801-715-6777

Utah State Library:
http://pioneer.utah.gov/research/guides/genealogy.html

Family Search has the following indexes that can be searched online for free:

Utah Death Certificates, 1904-1956:
https://familysearch.org/search/collection/1747615

Utah, Births and Christenings, 1892-1941:
https://familysearch.org/search/collection/1675542

Utah, County Marriages, 1887-1937:
https://familysearch.org/search/collection/1803977

Utah, Deaths and Burials, 1888-1946:
https://familysearch.org/search/collection/1675547

Utah, Marriages, 1887-1966:
https://familysearch.org/search/collection/1675546

Utah, Salt Lake County Birth Records, 1890-1915:
https://familysearch.org/search/collection/1464677

Utah, Salt Lake County Death Records, 1908-1949:
https://familysearch.org/search/collection/1459704

Census Records

Census records are among the most important genealogical documents for placing your ancestor in a particular place at a specific time. Like BDM records, they can also lead you to other ancestors, particularly those who were living under the authority of the head of household.

Family Search Family History Library – Utah census records 1850-1930

35 North West Temple Street
Salt Lake City, Utah, 84150
1-866-406-1830

Family History Library:
https://familysearch.org/locations/saltlakecity-library

The **Free Census Project** has transcribed many Utah indexes and new material is added daily

Free Census Project: http://usgwcensus.org/cenfiles/ut.htm

Access Genealogy – Utah county census records dating from 1860

Access Genealogy: http://www.accessgenealogy.com/census/utah-census-records.htm

African American Census Schedules Online – slave schedules, mortality schedules, slave-owners census

African American Census Schedules Online:
http://www.afrigeneas.com/aacensus/

Native Americans in Census Records (US National Archives):
http://www.archives.gov/research/census/native-americans/

<u>Utah Church Records</u>

Church and synagogue records are a valuable resource, especially for baptisms, marriages, and burials that took place before 1900. You will need to at least have an idea of your ancestor's religious denomination, and in most cases you will have to visit a brick and mortar establishment to view them.

Most church records are kept by the individual church, although in some denominations, records are placed in a regional archive or maintained at the diocesan level. Local Historical Societies are sometimes the repository for the state's older church records. Below are links archives that maintain church records, as well as a few databases that can be viewed online.The **Family History Library** contains many church records from a variety of denominations on microfilm.

Family History Library:
http://familysearch.org/learn/wiki/en/Family_History_Library

Central Repositories for Denominational Records

<u>Church of Jesus Christ of Latter-day Saints (Mormons)</u>

Early Mormon Church records for Utah can be found on film located at the LDS Family History Library in Salt Lake City and can be searched via the **Family History Library Catalog**

Family History Library Catalog:
https://familysearch.org/eng/Library/FHLC/frameset_fhlc.asp

The **Church History Library** has an even broader collection of historical church records than the Family History Library.
Church History Library
15 East North Temple
Salt Lake City, Utah 84150-1600
Phone: (801) 240-2272

Church History Library:
https://history.lds.org/?lang=eng#FlashPluginDetected

Episcopal

Diocese of Utah
80 South 300 East Street
Salt Lake City, Utah 84111
Phone: (801) 322-4131

Diocese of Utah: http://www.episcopal-ut.org/

Lutheran

Rocky Mountain District, LCMS
14334 E. Evans Ave
Aurora, CO 80014
Phone: (303) 695-8001
Fax: (303) 695-4047

Rocky Mountain District, LCMS: http://rm.lcms.org/

Presbyterian

Presbytery of Utah
342 West 200 South Street Suite 30
Salt Lake City, UT 84101
Phone: (801) 539-8446

Presbytery of Utah: http://www.pbyutah.org/

Westminster College Library
1840 South 1300 East
Salt Lake City, UT 84105
Phone: (801) 484-7651

Westminster College Library:
http://www.westminster.edu/library/library_overview.cfm

Presbyterian Historical Society
425 Lombard Street
Philadelphia, PA 19147
Telephone: 1-215-627-1852
Fax: 1-215-627-0509

Presbyterian Historical Society: http://www.history.pcusa.org/

Methodist

Iliff School of Theology
Ira J. Taylor Library Archives
2201 South University Blvd.
Denver, CO 80210
Phone: (303) 744-1287
Fax: (303) 744-3387

Ira J. Taylor Library Archives:
http://www.iliff.edu/index/learn/library/

United Methodist Church Rocky Mountain
2800 S. University Blvd.
Denver, CO 80710
Phone: (303) 733-3736
Fax: (303) 733-1730

United Methodist Church Rocky Mountain:
http://www.rmcumc.org/new/

Roman Catholic

Pastoral Center
Diocese of Salt Lake City
27 C Street
Salt Lake City, UT 84103
Phone: (801) 328-8641
Fax: (801) 328-9680
Archives extension: 304

Diocese of Salt Lake City: http://www.dioslc.org/contact-us

Utah Military Records

More than 40 million Americans have participated in some kind of war service since America was colonized. The chance of finding your ancestor amongst those records is exceptionally high. Military records can even reveal individuals who never actually served, such as those who registered for the two World Wars but were never called to duty.

Below are a number of links to websites and archives that contain Utah military records.

Utah State Archives – Service cards on Utah veterans of the Spanish American War, Mexican Boarder Campaign, and WWI; Large collection of Utah Territorial Militia records, Military Separation Forms and Benefit Records, Veterans' Case Files, Military discharges, Indian War Veterans' Fund Records, Discharged Veterans List, Philippine Insurrection Service Cards, Mexican Border Campaign Service Cards, Veterans' Educational Benefits Records, Veteran Burial Location Data, World War I Service Questionnaires, Selective Service Cards

300 S Rio Grande St
Salt Lake City, UT 84101
Tel: (801) 533-3535

Utah State Archives: http://www.archives.state.ut.us

Sons of Utah Pioneers – Mormon Battalion histories, American Revolution soldier lists, Pioneer Company lists

3301 East 2920 South
Salt Lake City, UT 84109
Toll-free Tel: 1-866-724-1847
LocalTel: 801-484-4441
Fax: 801-484-2067
E-mail: sup1847@gmail.com

Sons of Utah Pioneers: http://www.sonsofutahpioneers.org/

US Department of Veterans Affairs Nationwide Gravesite Locator – includes information on veterans and their family members buried in veterans and military cemeteries having a government grave marker.

US Department of Veterans Affairs Nationwide Gravesite Locator: http://gravelocator.cem.va.gov/

Family Search has the following indexes which are searchable online for free:

Utah, Veterans with Federal Service Buried in Utah, Territorial to 1966: https://familysearch.org/search/collection/1542862

Utah, Territorial Militia Records, 1849-1877: https://familysearch.org/search/collection/1462415

Utah, Indian War Service Affidavits, 1909-1917: https://familysearch.org/search/collection/1392781

You may also find your ancestor's military records in the following databases:

United States General Index to Pension Files, 1861-1934: https://familysearch.org/search/collection/1919699

United States Index to Service Records, War with Spain, 1898: https://familysearch.org/search/collection/1919583

United States Index to Indian Wars Pension Files, 1892-1926 – military pension records of soldiers who fought in the Indian Wars between 1817 and 1898

United States Index to Indian Wars Pension Files, 1892-1926: https://familysearch.org/search/collection/1979427

United States Registers of Enlistments in the U.S. Army, 1798-1914 - index of men who enlisted in the United States Army, 1798-1914.

United States Registers of Enlistments in the U.S. Army, 1798-1914: https://familysearch.org/search/collection/1880762

United States Mexican War Pension Index, 1887-1926 - index to Mexican War pension files for service between 1846 and 1848

United States Mexican War Pension Index, 1887-1926: https://familysearch.org/search/collection/1979390

Civil War Soldiers Service Records - Service records for both Union and Confederate soldiers indexed by soldier's name, rank, and unit.

Civil War Soldier Service Records: http://go.fold3.com/civilwar_records/

Utah Cemetery Records

As convenient as it is to search cemetery records online, keep in mind that there are a few disadvantages over visiting a cemetery in person. They are:

1. Tombstone information is not always accurately transcribed
2. The arrangement of the graves in a cemetery can be crucial as family members are often buried next to each other or in the same grave. This arrangement is not always preserved in the alphabetical indexes that are found online.

With that information in mind, the following websites have databases that can be searched online for Utah Cemetery records.

Utah State Archives – Cemetery records from many publicly owned cemeteries in Utah dating from 1850's to present

300 S Rio Grande St
Salt Lake City, UT 84101
Tel: (801) 533-3535

Utah State Archives: http://www.archives.state.ut.us

Utah State Library – Ogden City Cemetery records

250 North, 1950 West, Suite A
Salt Lake City, UT 84116-7901
801-715-6777

Utah State Library:
http://pioneer.utah.gov/research/guides/genealogy.html

Utah Tombstone Transcription Project - death and burial records

Utah Tombstone Transcription Project:
http://www.usgwtombstones.org/utah/utah.html

African American Cemeteries Online – African American, slave, and Native American cemetery records

African American Cemeteries Online: http://africanamericancemeteries.com/

Access Genealogy – database of Utah cemetery record transcriptions

Access Genealogy: http://www.accessgenealogy.com/cemetery/utah-cemeteries-records.htm

Find a Grave – over 100 million grave records can be searched on this site. Search can be conducted by name, location, or cemetery name.

Find a Grave: http://www.findagrave.com/

Interment.net - A free online database containing approximately 4 million cemetery records from around the world.

Interment.net: http://www.interment.net/

Billion Graves – as the name implies, you can search a billion records including headstone photos, transcriptions, cemetery records, and grave locations.

Billion Graves: http://billiongraves.com/pages/search/index.php#cemetery

Utah Obituaries

Obituaries can reveal a wealth about our ancestor and other relatives. You can search our **Utah Obituaries Listings** from hundreds of Utah newspapers online for free.

Utah Obituaries Listings: http://obituarieshelp.org/utah_newspaper_obituaries.html

Utah Wills and Probate Records

The documents found in a probate packet may include a complete inventory of a person's estate, newspaper entries, witness testimony, a copy of a will, list of debtors and creditors, names of executors or trustees, names of heirs. They can not only tell you about the ancestor you're currently researching, but lead to other ancestors.

Utah State Archives – County Probate Court Records, 1850-1896 (Minutes, Probate docket books, Probate record books, Record books, Administrators' record books, Guardians and executors records), State Distrcit Court Records, 1850-Present (Probate Registers, Probate Case Files, Probate Minute Books, Probate Record Books, Probate Registers Of Action, Wills)

300 S Rio Grande St
Salt Lake City, UT 84101
Tel: (801) 533-3535

Utah State Archives: http://www.archives.state.ut.us

Family Search has the following indexes that can be searched online for free:

Utah, Box Elder County Records, 1856-1960:
https://familysearch.org/search/collection/1935517

Utah, Cache County Records, 1861-1955:
https://familysearch.org/search/collection/1951443

Utah, Davis County Records, 1869-1953:
https://familysearch.org/search/collection/1922448

Utah, Probate Records, 1851-1961:
https://familysearch.org/search/collection/1916182

Utah, Tooele County Records, 1855-1956:
https://familysearch.org/search/collection/1992424

Utah Immigration and Naturalization Records

The naturalization process generated many types of records, including petitions, declarations of intention, and oaths of allegiance. These records can provide family historians with information such as a person's birth date and place of birth, immigration year, marital status, spouse information, occupation, witnesses' names and addresses, and more.

If your ancestor lived in or near a large city, or near a city where U.S. courts convened, you may find naturalization records in the **U.S. District Court** before 1906.

U.S. District Court:
http://www.uscourts.gov/FederalCourts/UnderstandingtheFederalCo
urts/DistrictCourts.aspx

For the rural areas of Utah, naturalization records may be found with the **County Clerk** in each county. Often the records were mixed in with other court proceedings making them difficult to locate. A few counties kept separate records for naturalization. After 1906, all naturalizations were handled in Federal District Courts.

County Clerks: http://www.utcourts.gov/directory/

Utah State Archives – Declaration of Intention Record Books, Certificates of Citizenship Record Book, Naturalization Record Books, Naturalization Records, Citizenship Certificate Stubs, dating from 1850's to present

300 S Rio Grande St
Salt Lake City, UT 84101
Tel: (801) 533-3535

Utah State Archives: http://www.archives.state.ut.us

Utah State Library – Emigration Registers, the Mormon Pioneer Overland Travel, 1847-1868 database - a searchable listing of individuals and companies in which Mormon pioneer emigrants traveled west to Utah from 1847 through 1868

250 North, 1950 West, Suite A
Salt Lake City, UT 84116-7901
801-715-6777

Utah State Library:
http://pioneer.utah.gov/research/guides/genealogy.html

Sons of Utah Pioneers – Shipping lists, Handcart pioneer lists, Perpetual Emigration Fund Emigrants

3301 East 2920 South
Salt Lake City, UT 84109
Toll-free Tel: 1-866-724-1847
LocalTel: 801-484-4441
Fax: 801-484-2067
E-mail: sup1847@gmail.com

Sons of Utah Pioneers: http://www.sonsofutahpioneers.org/

US National Archives – Immigration records, Naturalization records, Ship's Passenger lists

The National Archives and Records Administration
8601 Adelphi Road
College Park, MD 20740-6001
Tel: 1-866-272-6272; 1-86-NARA-NARAS

US National Archives: http://www.archives.gov/research/guide-fed-records/groups/085.html

Utah Native American Records

Regional Archives Rocky Mountain Region (Denver) - Indian Census Rolls

17101 Huron Street
Broomfield, CO 80023
Telephone:303-604-4740, or 303-407-5740
Fax: 303-407-5709

Regional Archives Rocky Mountain Region (Denver):
http://www.archives.gov/denver/public/genealogy.html

Access Genealogy – Utah Native American census records, tribal histories, and much more

Access Genealogy: http://www.accessgenealogy.com/native/utah-indian-tribes.htm

U.S. National Archives - information on American Indians who maintained their ties to Federally-recognized Tribes (1830-1970):
Website: http://www.archives.gov/research/native-americans/

Records of the Bureau of Indian Affairs (BIA) link to:
http://www.archives.gov/research/guide-fed-records/groups/075.html

American Indians Records Repository - records dating from the 1700s including trust, education and other historic Indian Affairs records

American Indian Records Repository
Meritex Enterprises
17501 West 98th Street
Lenexa, KS 66219
Phone: 913-888-0601

American Indians Records Repository:
http://www.doi.gov/ost/records_mgmt/american-indian-records-repository.cfm

Missing Matriarchs – Resources for Researching Female Utah Ancestors

Looking for female ancestors requires an adjustment of how we view traditional records sources. A woman's identity was often under that of her husband, and often individual records for them can be difficult to locate. The following resources are effective in locating female ancestors in Utah where traditional records may not reveal them.

Bibliographies

- *Audacious Women: Early British Mormon Immigrants,* Rebecca and Ralph Bartholomew (Signature Books, 1995)
- *Sunbonnet Sisters: True Stories of Mormon Women and Frontier Life,* Leonard J. and Susan Arrington Madsen (Bookcraft Press, 1981)
- *Mormon Sisters: Women in Early Utah,* Claudia Bushman (Utah State University Press, 1997)
- *Gathered in Tine: Utah Quilts and Their Makers, Settlement to 1950,* Kae Covington (University of Utah Press, 1997)
- *Trailing the Pioneers: A Guide to Utah's Emigrant Trails, 1829-1869,* Peter DeLafosse, (Utah State University Press, 1994)
- *Polygamy and the Frontier Mormon Women in Early Utah,* Lawrence Foster (Utah Historical Quarterly 50 (Summer 1982): 268-89

Selected Resources for Utah Women's History

Brigham Young University
Women's Research Institute
945 SWKT
Provo, UT 84602

Family History Library
35 North West Temple
Salt Lake City, UT 84150

Marriot Library
University of Utah
Salt Lake City, UT 84112

Merrill Library Special Collections
Utah State University
College Hill
Logan, UT 84321

Common Utah Surnames

The following surnames are among the most common in Utah and are also being currently researched by other genealogists. If you find your surname here, there is a chance that some research has already been performed on your ancestor.

ABLET, ABNER, ADAMS, ALDES, ALDOUS, ANDERSON, ANNAS, ASHCROFT, BALDRY, BALDWIN, BARKER, BARNABY, BATES, BEARSS, BEDDINGFIELD, BEDINGFIELD, BERRETT, BILLY, BIORNSEN, BRADFORD, BRANCH, BRODIE, BRUUS, BURGES, BURTON, CALVER, CARVER, CHRISTENSEN, CHRISTIANSEN, CLARK, CLEMENTS, CLUTTON, CROCKET, CROW, CROWE, DAHL, DAINES, DARRICOTT, DAVENPORT, DAVIS, DAY, DEWHURST, DOGGETT, DOWDLE, DYER, EBBESEN, EDWARDS, ELLIS, FENEX, FEVERYEAR, FEVIER, FIELDING, FISK, GALE, GAY, GAYNE, GERMANDSEN, GLOVER, GRACE, GRIFFIN, GROVES, GUNNING (GUNING), HADDOCK, HANSEN, HILL, HILLIER, HOWARD, HYMAS, JACKSON, JENOR, JENSEN, JOHN, JONES, KEELER, KENT, KING, KINGE, KNUDSEN, LAMB, LAMMONT, LAPHAM, LARSEN, LARWOOD, LEGGETT, LING, LOCKWOOD, MARKUSSEN, MARTIN, MAYHEW, MICHELSEN, MILLER, MORRIS, NAISH, NASH, NEIL, NEWMAN, NIELSEN, OATLEY, PARDEE, PARSONS, PEAKE, PEARCE, PEACE, PEDERSEN, PERCE, PERSE, PHENIX, PIERCE, PIRCE, PORTER, POUELSEN, POULSEN, PRATT, PRICTER, REDDISH, REEVE, ROCKWELL, ROGERS, ROSE OR ROUS, ROUSE, ROWSE, RUSH, RUSHE, SALTER, SAUNDERS, SAVAGE, SEAMAN, SEAMONS SILLETT, SIMONSEN, SMITH, SORENSEN, SPENCER, SPINK, ST. JOHN, STEVENSON, STOCKDALE, SUMMON, SUMMONS, SYER, THORKILDSEN, THORNE, TOWER, TRUSSON, TUCKER, TWYNE, TYE, WAIT, WALDRON, WALKER, WARD, WARNE, WATSON, WEBB, WEED, WHITE, WIGLEY, WILKENSON, WILKINSON, WITHE, WOODHEAD, WOOLEY, WOOLNOUGH, WRIGHT, YOUNG

About the Author

Gary L. Morris worked from 2009 to 2014 as a professional researcher for a major player in the genealogy field. After tracing his family lineage back to 1683, he found that genealogy could be an expensive undertaking. As such, has decided to publish these helpful guides to share the valuable free information he has discovered during his career to help others trace their family lineages as inexpensively as possible. An avid genealogist himself, he hopes you will find this guide factual, thorough, helpful, and most of all, effective in helping you to find your family members.

Notes

Notes

www.ingramcontent.com/pod-product-compliance
Lightning Source LLC
Chambersburg PA
CBHW070512290526
45790CB00003B/1205